JACK and Jill

Flip-Side Rhymes

From the point of view of JACK

by Christopher Harbo

illustrated by Colin Jack

raintree

a Capstone company — publishers for children

Jack and

Jill

went up the hill

to fetch
a pail
of water.

Jack fell down
and broke his crown,

and Jill came tumbling after.

10

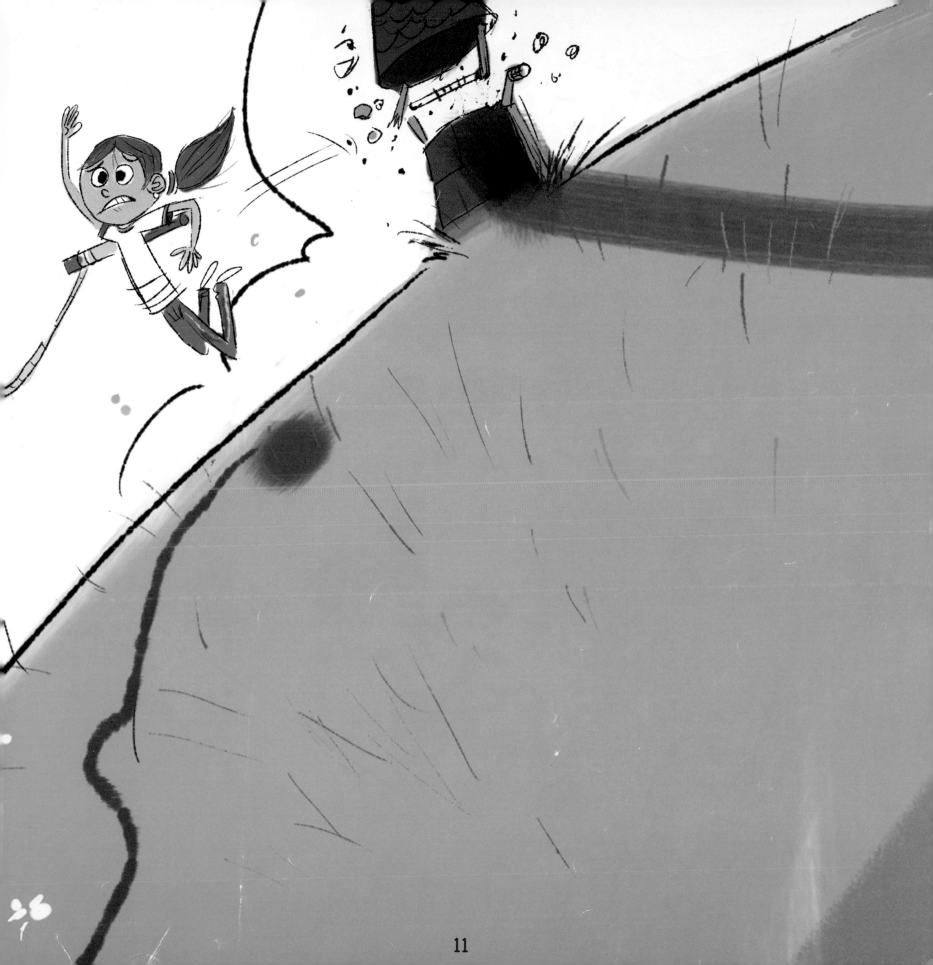

NOW **FLIP** THE BOOK
TO GET ANOTHER SIDE OF THE RHYME.

Raintree is an imprint of Capstone Global Library Limited. a company incorporated in England and Wales having its registered office at 64 Banbury Road. Oxford. OX2 7DY – Registered company number: 6695582

www.raintree.co.uk
myorders@raintree.co.uk

Text © Capstone Global Library Limited 2020
The moral rights of the proprietor have been asserted.

Editor: Gillia Olson
Designer: Ashlee Suker
Art Director: Nathan Gassman
Production Specialist: Laura Manthe
The illustrations in this book were created digitally.
Original illustrations © Capstone Global Library Limited 2020
Originated by Capstone Global Library Ltd
Printed and bound in India

ISBN 978 1 4747 9056 7
24 23 22 21 20
10 9 8 7 6 5 4 3 2 1

British Library Cataloguing in Publication Data
A full catalogue record for this book is available from the British Library.

NOW FLIP THE BOOK
TO GET ANOTHER SIDE OF THE RHYME.

other titles in this series:

Humpty DUMPTY
FLIP-Side Rhymes

Little BO PEEP
FLIP-Side Rhymes

Little Miss MUFFET
FLIP-Side Rhymes

black and blue!

and now they're both

But then she stumbled
and down they
tumbled,

so she kicked him
with her shoe.

6

as they climbed the hill,

Jack shoved Jill

JACK
and
Jill

FLIP-Side
Rhymes

From the point
of view of Jill

by christopher Harbo

illustrated by colin Jack

raintree

a Capstone company — publishers for children